St. Patrick's Day Crafts

by Ann Malaspina • illustrated by Mernie Gallagher-Cole

The Child's World®
childsworld.com

Published by The Child's World®
1980 Lookout Drive • Mankato, MN 56003-1705
800-599-READ • www.childsworld.com

Acknowledgments
The Child's World®: Mary Swensen, Publishing Director
Red Line Editorial: Editorial direction and production
The Design Lab: Design

Photographs ©: iStockphoto, 4

ISBN 9781503808188
LCCN 2015958128

Printed in the United States of America
Mankato, MN
June, 2016
PA02298

About the Author
Ann Malaspina is an author of children's books. Her great-great grandfather was born in Ireland. She plays Irish music on her fiddle. Malaspina likes to travel, especially to Ireland.

About the Illustrator
Mernie Gallagher-Cole is an artist living in West Chester, Pennsylvania. She has illustrated many books, games, and puzzles for children. She loves crafts and tries to be creative every day.

Table of Contents

Introduction to St. Patrick's Day

People around the world celebrate St. Patrick's Day on March 17. They honor St. Patrick. He was born in the United Kingdom. Pirates took him to Ireland when he was a boy. They sold him as a slave. St. Patrick cared for the sheep in the fields. He was a shepherd. After six years, he escaped and went home.

St. Patrick returned to Ireland around 400 AD. He helped the Irish people. He was humble and brave.

A group of Irish dancers performs at the New York City St. Patrick's Day parade.

For these reasons, St. Patrick became Ireland's **patron saint**. March 17, 461, is the day of his death.

St. Patrick's Day is a national holiday in Ireland. People stay home from work. Schools are closed, too. Parades fill the streets with Irish flags and music. Some people go to church to pray. March 17 is a day to celebrate what it means to be Irish.

You do not have to be Irish to celebrate. People around the world eat Irish food. This includes soda bread, corned beef, and cabbage. They wear a **shamrock**. This is a special Irish plant. People may even do an Irish dance. Let's celebrate together by making crafts.

Shamrock Card

Pin a shamrock on your hat or coat for St. Patrick's Day. The small green plant is a **symbol** of the holiday. It has three leaves on each stem. Each leaf is shaped similarly to a heart. Some people paint one on their face to celebrate the day. Make a shamrock card for someone special.

MATERIALS

- ☐ Scissors
- ☐ Green construction paper
- ☐ Pencil
- ☐ White card stock paper
- ☐ Glue
- ☐ Pen

STEPS

1. Using a scissors, cut the green construction paper into four equal squares. Fold three of the squares in half. Set the fourth square aside.

2. Using a pencil, draw half a heart along the fold of the three squares. Then cut the hearts out. Be careful not to cut the folded edges. Unfold the paper to see the hearts.

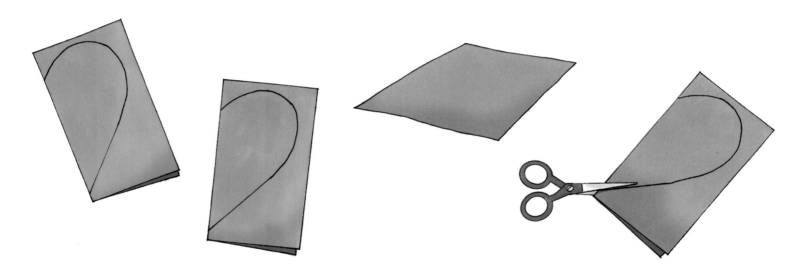

3. Take the fourth green paper square from Step 1. Cut out a short, narrow rectangle. This will be the stem.

4. Fold the white card stock paper in half. Fold it in half again. This will be your card.

5. Place the three hearts and stem on the front of the card. Form them into a shamrock. Glue each piece to the card. Let it dry.

6. Once the card is dry, open it up. Using your pen, write a St. Patrick's Day message.

Rainbow Wind Sock

Ireland is an island near England. It is often cloudy and rainy. A rainbow may form when the sun peeks from behind the clouds. Make a rainbow wind sock. This will brighten your St. Patrick's Day. This wind sock is made of paper. Don't let it get wet in the rain!

MATERIALS

- ☐ Crayons
- ☐ One sheet of construction paper, any color
- ☐ Glue
- ☐ Tissue paper, many colors
- ☐ Scissors
- ☐ Hole punch
- ☐ String

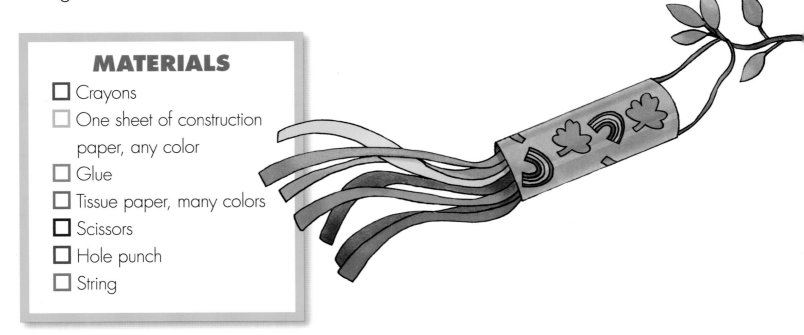

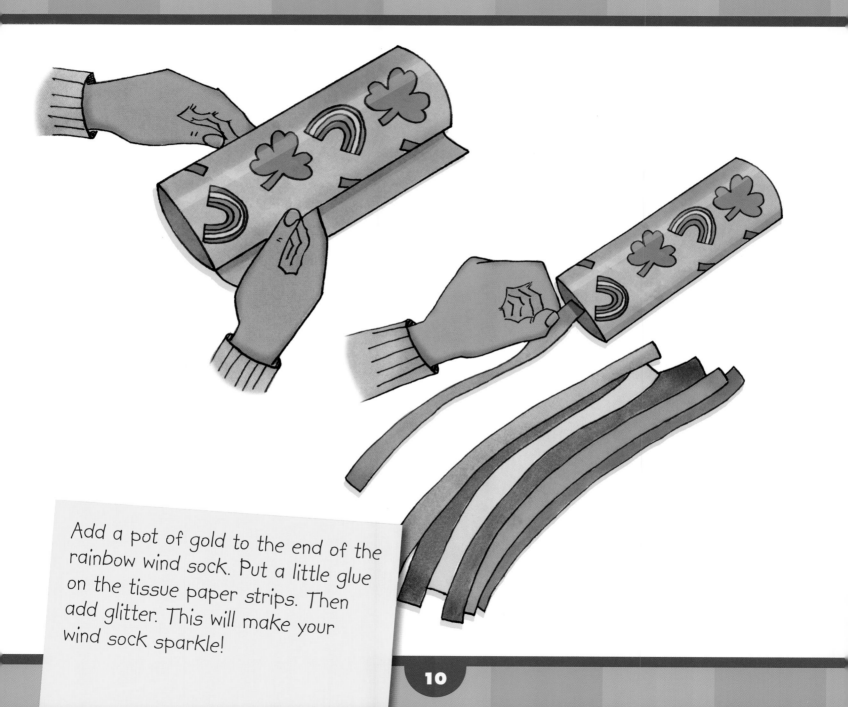

Add a pot of gold to the end of the rainbow wind sock. Put a little glue on the tissue paper strips. Then add glitter. This will make your wind sock sparkle!

STEPS

1. Take crayons and a sheet of construction paper. Draw shamrocks and rainbows on the paper.

2. Roll the paper into a long tube. Glue the long edges on top of each other to close the tube. Let it dry.

3. Cut the tissue paper into long strips with a scissors. These strips will flutter in the wind. Glue the strips around the bottom inside of the tube. Use as many strips as you want.

4. At the top of the tube, punch two holes across from each other.

5. Cut a piece of string. Push one end of the string through a hole and make a loop. Tie a double knot to hold the loop. Do the same with the string in the other hole.

6. Hang your wind sock using the string. Everyone can enjoy the bright colors of the rainbow.

Cardboard Irish Harp

Some people play the Irish **harp** on St. Patrick's Day. It is an old instrument. The harp is made of wood and metal strings. People pluck the strings to make music. The harp is the official symbol of Ireland. Join the fun with your own cardboard harp.

MATERIALS

- ☐ Picture of an Irish harp
- ☐ Thin sturdy cardboard
- ☐ Pencil
- ☐ Scissors
- ☐ Hole punch
- ☐ Gold string

STEPS

1. With an adult's help, find a picture of an Irish harp online. Draw an outline of a harp on the cardboard using a pencil. Make sure the sides of the harp are wide enough to punch holes in.

2. Cut out the harp with scissors.

3. Punch holes in a line across the bottom of the harp using a hole punch. Then punch holes across the top of the harp.

Decorate your harp to make it your own. Paint the harp before you add the strings. Use glue and glitter for sparkles. Draw shamrocks or rainbows.

4. Thread the gold string through the top right hole. Make a loop and tie a double knot to hold the string in place.

5. Start threading the string from the top right hole to the bottom right hole.

6. Then thread the string through the second bottom hole and up to the second top hole.

7. Repeat these motions until the string is through all the holes. Move from right to left.

8. Tie the string in the last hole with a loop and a double knot. Your harp is now complete.

Paper Plate Leprechaun

Long ago, people in Ireland told stories about leprechauns. Leprechauns look like little men. They have long beards and tall hats. They sing, dance, and make shoes. Leprechauns like to trick people. They can also be kind. Make your own leprechaun out of a paper plate this St. Patrick's Day.

MATERIALS

- [ ] 9-inch (23-cm) paper plate
- [ ] Orange paint
- [ ] Paintbrush
- [ ] Scissors
- [ ] Black marker
- [ ] Two sheets of green construction paper
- [ ] Sheet of black construction paper
- [ ] Ruler
- [ ] Sheet of yellow construction paper
- [ ] Glue

STEPS

1. Turn the paper plate upside down. Paint the outer rim orange using a paintbrush. Leave about one-fourth of the rim unpainted for the leprechaun's hat. Let the paint dry.

2. When the paint is dry, cut out small strips around the rim with a scissors. This style makes the leprechaun's beard.

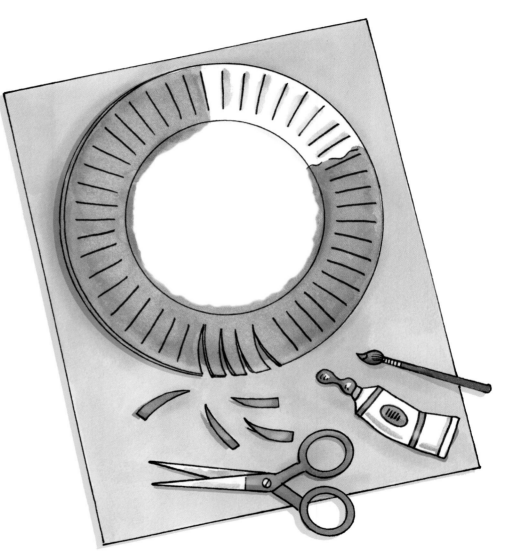

3. Now you can make his face. Draw his mouth near the center of the plate with the black marker.

4. Cut out a circle nose from the green paper. Then cut out two eyes from the black paper. Glue the nose and eyes on the paper plate.

5. Next make the hat. Use a ruler to measure and cut out a green rectangle. It should be 9 inches (23 cm) long by 6 inches (15 cm) wide.

6. Cut out a hat brim from the green paper. It should be 2 inches (5.1 cm) long by 9 inches (23 cm) wide. Glue the brim to the bottom of the hat.

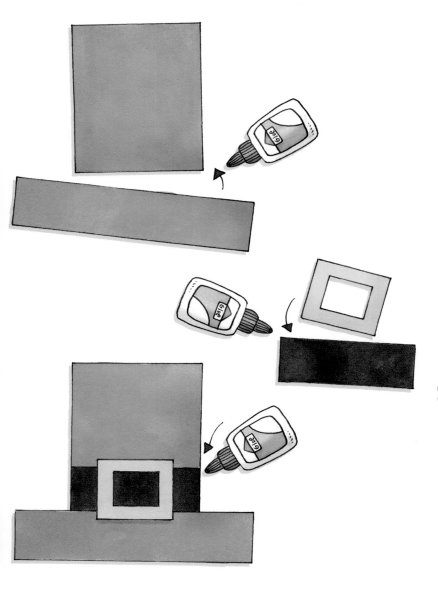

7. Make the hatband next. Measure and cut out a black rectangle that is 1 inch (2.5 cm) long and 6 inches (15 cm) wide.

8. Measure and cut out a yellow square. This is for the buckle. The square should be 2 inches (5.1 cm) by 2 inches (5.1 cm). Fold the square in half. Cut out an inner square. This will not be used.

9. Glue the buckle to the hatband. Then glue the band to the hat. Finally, glue the hat to the top of the plate. Now your leprechaun is done!

Pot of Gold Bookmarks

Many stories are told about St. Patrick. Some are true. Others are not. One story is that he drove the snakes out of Ireland. But scientists say Ireland never had snakes. You can make a bookmark for your favorite St. Patrick's Day storybook. Decorate it with a harp, a pot of gold, or other objects. Then open your book and start reading!

MATERIALS

- ☐ Ruler
- ☐ Scissors
- ☐ White or light green stock paper
- ☐ Brown, yellow, and green paint
- ☐ Paper plate
- ☐ Rag
- ☐ Black marker
- ☐ Small paintbrush
- ☐ Hole punch
- ☐ Green ribbon

STEPS

1. Using a ruler and scissors, measure and cut the card stock into rectangles for the bookmarks. A good size is 2 to 3 inches (5.1 to 7.6 cm) wide and 6 inches long (15 cm).

2. Pour a large spoonful of each paint color on a paper plate.

3. Dip your thumb in the brown paint. Make a thumbprint on the card. This is the pot. Use the rag to keep your hands clean.

4. Use the black marker to draw a handle on the pot.

5. Dip your pinky finger in yellow paint. Then press it to the paper above the pot. This will be the gold in the pot.

6. Add a shamrock to the bookmark. Use your pinky finger to make three green leaves. Paint a stem below the leaves using a small paintbrush.

7. Punch a hole at the top of the bookmark.

8. Tie a green ribbon through the hole.

9. Repeat steps 3 through 8 on the other bookmarks.

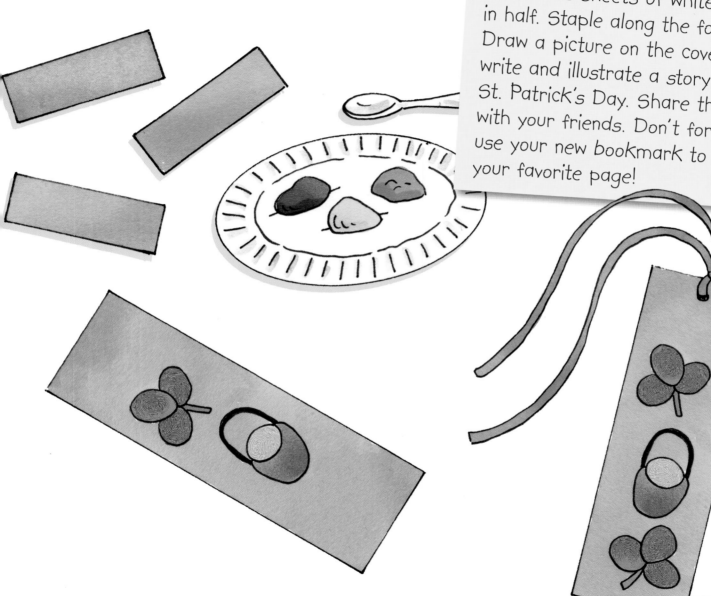

Create your own holiday book. Fold three sheets of white paper in half. Staple along the fold. Draw a picture on the cover. Then write and illustrate a story about St. Patrick's Day. Share the book with your friends. Don't forget to use your new bookmark to mark your favorite page!

Glossary

harp (HARP) The harp is a stringed instrument played with your fingers. People play the harp on St. Patrick's Day.

patron saint (PAY-truhn SAYNT) A patron saint is a person who is believed to protect a place or group of people. St. Patrick is the patron saint of Ireland.

shamrock (SHAM-rok) The shamrock is a small plant with three leaves on each stem. The shamrock is one of Ireland's favorite plants.

symbol (SIM-buhl) A symbol is used to represent something else. The harp is the symbol for the Republic of Ireland.

To Learn More

IN THE LIBRARY

Keogh, Josie. *St. Patrick's Day*. New York: PowerKids, 2013.

Lindeen, Mary. *St. Patrick's Day*. Chicago: Norwood House, 2015.

Lynette, Rachel. *Let's Throw a St. Patrick's Day Party!* New York: PowerKids, 2012.

ON THE WEB

Visit our Web site for links about St. Patrick's Day Crafts:

childsworld.com/links

Note to Parents, Teachers, and Librarians:
We routinely verify our Web links to make sure they are safe and active
sites. So encourage your readers to check them out!

Index